THIS BOOK BELONGS TO

_______________________________

FOR MY FATHER LEO, AND
BEST FRIEND
SETH

IN A BUSTLING TERMITE COLONY NESTLED DEEP IN THE TOWN OF WILLOWBROOK IN THE HEART OF THE SPRAWLING FOREST.

TERMITE IN THE COLONY, AS HE HARBORED A DEEP-SEATED SECRET

THERE LIVED A YOUNG TERMITE NAMED TIMMY. TIMMY WAS UNLIKE OTHER TERMITES IN THE COLONY, AS HE HARBORED A DEEP-SEATED SECRET.

THAT DEEP-SEATED DESIRE WAS TO BECOME A CARPENTER.

WHILE MOST TERMITES WERE CONTENT TO MUNCH ON WOOD AND BUILD INTRICATE TUNNELS WITHIN THE EARTH.

TIMMY YEARNED FOR MORE. HE WANTED TO CREATE BEAUTIFUL WOODEN MASTERPIECES THAT ALL WOULD ADMIRE.

DESPITE HIS PASSION FOR CARPENTRY, TIMMY'S PARENTS WERE SKEPTICAL OF HIS DREAMS...

THEY BELIEVED THAT AS A TERMITE,
HIS PLACE WAS SIMPLY TO EAT
WOOD AND CONTRIBUTE TO THE
COLONY IN THAT WAY!!

HIS FATHER WOULD SAY STERNLY.

YOU WERE BORN A TERMITE.

TIMMY, YOU CANNOT CHANGE
YOUR DESTINY.

BUT TIMMY REFUSED TO BE DISCOURAGED. HE WOULD SPEND HOURS PORING OVER CARPENTRY BOOKS BORROWED FROM THE NEARBY HUMAN VILLAGE.

STUDYING THE INTRICACIES OF WOODWORKING AND DREAMING OF THAT DAY WHEN HE COULD CREATE HIS OWN PIECES.

IT WAS DURING ONE OF THESE LATE-NIGHT STUDY SESSIONS THAT INSPIRATION STRUCK HIM.

AS TIMMY FLIPPED THROUGH A BOOK ON WOODWORKING TECHNIQUES, HE CAME ACROSS A CHAPTER ON CARVIN UTENSILS OUT OF WOOD.

AN IDEA BEGAN TO FORM IN HIS MIND.

WHAT IF HE COULD USE HIS CARPENTRY SKILLS TO MAKE FORKS AND KNIVES OUT OF DIFFERENT TYPES OF WOOD? THIS WAS, INSTEAD OF FAMILY'S FURNITURE, THE TERMITES COULD FEAST ON THE UTENSILS HE CREATED.

EXCITED BY HIS NEWFOUND PLAN, TIMMY ENROLLED IN A CARPENTRY SCHOOL LOCATED ON THE OUTSKIRTS OF THE FOREST.

HIS CLASSMATES, "ALL HUMANS," WERE INITIALLY SKEPTICAL OF THE TINY TERMITE IN THEIR MIST. BUT TIMMY SHOWCASED HIS SKILLS AND DEDICATION, THEY BEGAN TO RESPECT HIM FOR HIS TALENT.

DESPITE HIS SUCCESS AT SCHOOL, TIMMY STILL FACED RESISTANCE FROM HIS PARENTS.

TIMMY REMAINED UNCONVINCED THAT A TERMITE COULD EXCEL AS A CARPENTER. DETERMINED TO PROVE THEM WRONG.

TIMMY POURED ALL HIS ENERGY AND CREATIVITY INTO HIS CRAFT.

HE EXPERIMENTED WITH DIFFERENT TYPES OF WOOD, FROM PINE TO OAK TO MAHOGANY.

CREATING STUNNING PLATES, FORKS, AND KNIVES THAT SHOWCASED HIS SKILLS

ONE DAY, TIMMY PRESENTED HIS LATEST MASTERPIECE, AN INTRICATELY CARVED SALAD BOWL MADE FROM CHERRY WOOD.

TO HIS PARENTS, THEY WERE FINALLY WON OVER. TEARS FILLED HIS FATHER'S EYES AS HE GAZED AT HIS SON'S HANDIWORK.

"I NEVER THOUGHT,
TIMMY, YOU COULD
ACHIEVE SUCH
GREATNESS," HIS FATHER
WHISPERED INTO HIS EAR.

FROM THAT DAY ON, TIMMY
WAS HAILED AS A HERO IN THE
TERMITE COLONY.

AS A TESTAMENT TO WHAT
ONE DETERMINED TERMITE
COULD ACHIEVE.

AS THE YEARS PASSED, TIMMY'S REPUTATION AS A SKILLED CARPENTER SPREAD FAR AND WIDE. HE BECAME RENOWNED FOR HIS INTRICATE WOOD CREATION.

WHICH WERE SOUGHT AFTER BY HUMANS AND TERMITES ALIKE.

BUT DEEP DOWN. TIMMY KNEW
THAT HIS GREATEST
ACCOMPLISHMENT WAS NOT IN THE
PIECES HE CREATED BUT IN PROVING
TO HIMSELF AND HIS PARENTS.

THAT HE WAS MORE THAN JUST A
SIMPLE TERMITE

AND SO, THE TALE OF
TIMMY, THE TERMITE
CARPENTER, BECAME A
LEGEND IN THE FOREST.

INSPIRING GENERATIONS OF YOUNG TERMITES TO FOLLOW THEIR DREAMS AND NEVER GIVE UP

NO MATTER HOW IMPOSSIBLE THEY MAY SEEM.

ANYTHING IS POSSIBLE!

EVEN FOR A TINY TERMITE NAMED TIMMY WITH BIG DREAMS.

# TIMMY

I HOPE YOU WILL ENJOY READING MY STORY OF "TIMMY THE TERMITE CHARPENTE" AND MY HOPE IS YOU SHARE IT FOR GENERATIONS TO COME!

PAUL &
TIMMY TERMITE

PAUL B. BOLDUC IS A FREELANCE DESIGNER, KNOW FOR HIS OUT OF THE BOX APPROACH.  DOING MANY PROJECTS FOR MANY GLOBAL COMAPLIES, HE ALSO HAS MANY OTHER TALANTS UNDER HIS BELT AMONG SOME ARE WORKING WITH OTHER HAND BAG DESIGNERS IN THEIR PROJECT COLOBRATIONS. HIS SOCIAL MEDIA ACCOUNTS ARE FOLLOWED BY MANY OF WELL KNOWN IN THE FASHION WORLD.  NOW NEW AUTHOR, AND OVER ALL CREATIVE PERSON!